Gatherings
For company, everyday dinners and special occasions

GOOD FOOD, GOOD FRIENDS, GOOD GATHERINGS

Front cover
Amaretto spread

© Copyright 2007 Kate M. Semenchuk
All rights reserved. No part of this publication may be reproduced, stored in a retrieval system, or transmitted, in any form or by any means, electronic, mechanical, photocopying, recording, or otherwise, without the written prior permission of the author.

Photography by Doug Thordarson, Tanna Rusk, Kate Semenchuk

Styling by Darlene Skaritko, Carolyn Kawaleski, Sharon Thordarson, Linda Kehler, Kate Semenchuk

Edited by Darlene Skaritko, Ali Brown, Kate Semenchuk

Note for Librarians: A cataloguing record for this book is available from Library and Archives Canada at www.collectionscanada.ca/amicus/index-e.html
ISBN 1-4251-1649-3

Printed in Victoria, BC, Canada. Printed on paper with minimum 30% recycled fibre. Trafford's print shop runs on "green energy" from solar, wind and other environmentally-friendly power sources.

Offices in Canada, USA, Ireland and UK

Book sales for North America and international:
Trafford Publishing, 6E–2333 Government St.,
Victoria, BC V8T 4P4 CANADA
phone 250 383 6864 (toll-free 1 888 232 4444)
fax 250 383 6804; email to orders@trafford.com
Book sales in Europe:
Trafford Publishing (UK) Limited, 9 Park End Street, 2nd Floor
Oxford, UK OX1 1HH UNITED KINGDOM
phone +44 (0)1865 722 113 (local rate 0845 230 9601)
facsimile +44 (0)1865 722 868; info.uk@trafford.com
Order online at:
trafford.com/07-0053

10 9 8 7 6 5 4 3 2

Thank You

The first thing I would like to do is say thank you. Thank you to my family and friends for believing in me. Thank you to my test tasters and sanity savers for everything you have done. Thank you guys for all your tech support. I learned a lot from you. Love you all and happy cooking.

Good food, good friends, good gatherings,

Kate

Table of Contents

Appetizers 7
Salads. 38
Soups 52
Vegetables 67
Pasta 80
Meats 89

Appetizers

Taco Dip

2 cups sour cream
1 pkg. cream cheese
2 tsp. mayonnaise
1 pkg. taco seasoning
shredded lettuce
chopped tomato
grated cheddar cheese

Mix the first four ingredients. Refrigerate a few hours. Spread into a quiche pan. Top with lettuce, then tomatoes and sprinkle with cheese.

BBQ Water Chestnuts

1 can whole water chestnuts
bacon
1 cup ketchup
¾ cup brown sugar

Wrap one whole chestnut in ½ slice bacon. Secure with a toothpick. Bake at 250 F for 1 hour. Drain off fat. Mix ketchup and brown sugar. Pour over chestnuts. Bake at 250 F for 1 hour.

Hot Pumpernickel Dip

2 pkg. cream cheese
1 cup miracle whip
1 cup shredded cheese
½ tsp. garlic powder
1 tsp. dill
½ cup green onions
¾ lb. bacon

Cook bacon crisp. Mix everything together. Put in hollowed out loaf of pumpernickel. Wrap in tin foil. Bake for 2 hours at 350 F.

Cheeseball

1 pkg. cream cheese
3 cups cheddar cheese, shredded
¼ cup sour cream
¼ cup green onions chopped
3 slices bacon
Dash worcestershire
Dash tabasco
¾ cup chopped walnuts
¼ cup chopped cherries

Mix everything but the cherries and walnuts. Roll into a ball. Mix walnuts and cherries. Roll cheese ball in cherry mixture. Refrigerate. Serve with crackers.

Vegetable Pizza

2 pkg. crescent rolls
1 pkg. cream cheese
½ cup miracle whip
½ cup ranch dressing
½ tsp. garlic powder
½ tsp. onion powder
¼ cup grated carrots
¼ cup chopped cauliflower
¼ cup chopped celery
¼ cup chopped broccoli
¼ cup green onions
1 cup grated cheese

Press crescent dough into large cookie sheet. Bake at 375 F for 10 minutes. Mix cream cheese, miracle whip, ranch dressing, garlic powder and onion powder. Beat until smooth. Spread on cooled base. Add vegetables. Top with grated cheese.

Spinach and Artichoke Dip

1 small onion, chopped
2 cloves garlic, chopped
1 pkg. spinach thawed and drained
1 can artichokes, chopped and reserve 1 tbsp. liquid
1 pkg. cream cheese
½ cup milk
¾ cup sour cream
½ cup parmesan cheese
1 ½ cups mozzarella cheese

Sauté onion and garlic in artichoke liquid until tender. Add the spinach and sauté until the liquid has evaporated. Add artichokes, cream cheese and milk. Stir until the cream cheese melts. Add the sour cream, parmesan cheese and ½ cup mozzarella cheese. Transfer to a pie plate and sprinkle with remaining mozzarella cheese. Bake at 350F for 30 minutes or until bubbly and golden.

Guacamole

4 avocados, peeled
¼ cup lemon juice
½ cup mayonnaise
¼ cup chopped onion
1 tsp. chili powder
½ tsp. garlic powder
¼ tsp. cayenne
1 tsp. salt
¼ tsp. pepper

Peel and chop avocados. Put everything in a blender. Blend until smooth. Refrigerate until serving. This freezes well.

Baked Bruschetta

3 tomatoes, seeded and dried off.
1 ½ cups mozzarella cheese
1 ½ tsp. basil
1 ½ tsp. oregano
½ cup miracle whip
1 baguette

Finely chop tomato. Add cheese, basil, oregano and miracle whip. Stir well. Place on sliced baguette. Bake at 350 F until cheese is bubbly.

Roasted Onion and Pepper Dip

1 red pepper
1 onion
4 cloves garlic
1 tbsp. olive oil
¾ cup feta cheese
½ cup sour cream
½ cup mayonnaise
1 tbsp. lemon juice
¼ tsp. salt
¼ tsp. pepper

Cut onion and pepper in chunks, add oil and garlic. Bake at 350 for 40 minutes. In a blender mix feta, sour cream and mayonnaise. Add lemon juice, salt and pepper. Blend until smooth. Add pepper, onion and garlic. Blend until smooth and chill.

Cheddar Dill Loaf

2 pkg. cream cheese
1 tub imperial cheese
½ cup sour cream
½ cup mayonnaise
2 tbsp. dried onion
1 ½ tsp. dill
1 tsp. garlic
½ lb. cooked bacon
1 loaf French bread

Soften cream cheese. Add imperial cheese sour cream, mayonnaise, onion, dill and garlic. Beat until smooth. Stir in bacon. Cut top from French bread. Pull out insides and stuff with filling. Replace lid and wrap in foil. Bake 2 hours at 250F.

Parmesan Ham Swirls

1 egg
½ pkg. puff pastry
¼ cup parmesan cheese
¼ tsp. cayenne pepper
10 thin slices deli honey ham
1 tbsp. water
1 tbsp. butter

Beat egg and water. Roll puff pastry into a 12x14 rectangle. Cut in half lengthwise. Brush half with butter and place second strip on top. Brush top with egg. Mix ½ the parmesan cheese and cayenne. Sprinkle over egg. Cover with ham. Roll like a jelly roll. Pinch to seal. Slice and place on a greased pan. Brush with egg and sprinkle with rest of parmesan cheese. Bake at 400F for 12-14 minutes.

Cherry Puffs

2 cups grated cheddar cheese
½ cup margarine softened
1 cup flour
¼ tsp. salt
½ tsp. paprika
¼ cup water
48 glazed cherries

Blend cheese with butter and water. Add flour, salt and paprika. Mix well. Mold 1 teaspoon around each cherry. Freeze or refrigerate up to 10 days. Bake at 400 F for 15 minutes.

Kahlua Dip

- 1 pkg. cream cheese
- 1 small carton cool whip
- 2/3 cup brown sugar
- 1/3 cup kahlua
- 1 carton sour cream

Whip cream cheese until smooth. Fold in cool whip. Add brown sugar, Kahlua and sour cream. Mix well. Refrigerate over night.

Hot Broccoli Dip

1 cup broccoli
2 tbsp. minced onion
¼ cup parmesan cheese
3-4 cloves garlic
1 cup cheddar cheese
½ cup sour cream
½ cup mayonnaise
1/8 tsp. pepper

Mix all the ingredients together. Put in an oven proof dish and bake at 375F until bubbly. Serve on a baguette.

Hot Artichoke Dip

- 1 pkg. cream cheese
- 1 can artichoke hearts drained and chopped
- ½ cup mayonnaise
- ½ cup parmesan cheese
- 1 clove garlic chopped.

Mix everything and put into a pie plate. Bake at 350F for 20-25 minutes. Serve with crackers or a baguette.

Cheddar Beer Spread

2 cups old cheddar cheese, shredded
½ pkg. cream cheese, softened
¼ cup flat beer
2 tbsp. plain yogurt
1 tbsp. Dijon mustard
½ tsp. Worcestershire sauce
1 clove garlic, minced
hot pepper sauce
pepper

Beat together cheeses. Add beer, yogurt, mustard, and Worcestershire sauce. Add hot pepper sauce and pepper to taste. Mix well.

Spinach Dip

2 cups mayonnaise
1 cup sour cream
1 pkg. vegetable soup mix
4 chopped green onions
1 pkg. frozen chopped spinach

Mix and chill.

Coconut Dip

1 cup whipping cream
½ pkg. cream cheese
1 cup icing sugar
1 tsp. almond extract
1 cup coconut

Whip cream. In separate bowl, beat cream cheese, icing sugar and almond extract. Fold in whipped cream and coconut. Chill. Serve with fruit.

Baked Cream Cheese

1 pkg. crescent roll dough
1 pkg. cream cheese
½ tsp. dill
¼ cup fried onions
1 egg yolk
1 sprinkle seasoned salt

Unroll dough and press together at the seams. Sprinkle ½ the dill and ½ the onions on the cream cheese. Put the dill side down on the dough. Sprinkle the rest of the dill, and onions on the cream cheese. Add a light sprinkle of seasoned salt on top. Wrap the dough around the cream cheese and seal. Place on a greased cookie sheet. Brush with egg yolk. Bake at 350 F 15-18 minutes until brown. Serve with crackers.

Brie en Croute

1 wheel brie
½ pkg. puff pastry, thawed
1 egg yolk

Roll out puff pastry. Wrap brie in pastry and brush with egg yolk. Bake at 350F until golden.

Peanut Butter Dip

¼ cup peanut butter
3 tbsp. honey
2 tbsp. milk
½ cup miracle whip

Combine peanut butter and honey. Gradually add milk. Add miracle whip. Blend well. Chill. Serve with fruit.

Bacon Log

½ pound sharp cheese
8-10 slices uncooked bacon
½ tsp. Worcestershire
2 small onions
1 tsp. dry mustard
2 tsp. mayonnaise

Put cheese, Worcestershire, onions, dry mustard and mayonnaise in a blender. Mix well. Roll into a log about 1 ½ inches wide. Wrap bacon around the log. Freeze. When ready to serve, place in oven under the broiler until the bacon is ready. Serve with bread rounds or crackers.

Chestnut Surprises

2- 8 ounce cans whole water chestnuts
½ cup butter
2 cups sharp cheese
2 tbsp. sesame seeds
½ tsp. garlic salt
½ tsp. paprika
pinch cayenne
1 ½ cups flour

Drain chestnuts and let dry. Beat butter and cheese. Add seeds, salt, paprika, cayenne and beat. Work in flour. Mold 1 tablespoon around each chestnut. Cover and chill or freeze.
Chilled – Bake 425 F for 15-20 minutes.
Frozen – Bake 400 F for 30-45 minutes.

Bacon Dip

½ cup miracle whip
½ cup sour cream
1 cup mozzarella, shredded
½ tsp. onion powder
½ tsp. garlic powder
¼ cup parmesan cheese
1/3 cup crumbled bacon

Mix all together and serve with crackers or bread.

Hot Spinach Loaf

1 loaf French bread
¼ cup cooked bacon
1 pkg. frozen spinach
2 pkg. cream cheese
1 cup mayonnaise
salt and pepper
1 cup grated cheddar cheese
2 tsp. dill
¾ cup chopped green onions
1 clove minced garlic

Cut the loaf making a lid and bottom. Cut bread pieces out. Mix the rest of the ingredients together. Fill loaf bowl with filling. Put bread lid on. Wrap in tin foil and bake 350 F for 2 hours.

Mozzarella Dip

2 cups mayonnaise
1 cup sour cream
1 cup mozzarella cheese
2 tbsp. Parmesan cheese
1 tbsp. minced onion
1 tsp. sugar
1 tsp. salt
1 tsp. seasoned salt

Mix and chill. Serve with baguettes or crackers.

Cheese Sticks

½ cup butter
3 ounces sharp cheese
1 egg yolk
1 cup flour
¼ tsp. salt
1/8 tsp. cayenne

Cream butter and cheese together. Add the egg yolk. Mix flour, salt and cayenne together. Add to mixture. Chill dough and then roll to ¼ inch on floured surface. Cut in strips. Bake at 350F for 15 minutes.

Caramel Apple Brie

1 large apple peeled, cored and chopped
½ cup pecan pieces
1/3 cup brown sugar
2 tbsp. Kahlua
1 wheel Brie (about 2 pounds, rind left on)

Mix apple, pecans, brown sugar and Kahlua. Put on top of brie. Bake at 325F for 10-15 minutes or until topping is bubbly and cheese is softened.

Amaretto Spread

1 pkg. cream cheese
¼ cup amaretto
1 pkg. slivered almonds
2 tbsp. butter

Sauté almonds in the butter. Soften cream cheese and blend in amaretto. Form a ball and roll in almonds.

Cashew Wafers

1 lb. grated sharp cheddar cheese
½ lb. butter
salt to taste
¼ tsp. cayenne
2 cups flour divided
2 cups dry roasted cashews finely chopped
paprika or onion powder

Mix cheese until creamy. Add butter and continue beating. Add salt, pepper and 3 tablespoons of flour. Blend well. Continue adding flour until mixture becomes a soft dough and can be rolled into balls. Add nuts. Flour your hands. Roll small balls and flatten with a fork. Bake at 325F for 20-25 minutes. Sprinkle with paprika or onion powder when hot.

Bacon Cheese Ball

1 ¼ cup whole almonds
1 pkg. cream cheese
½ cup mayonnaise
slice crumbled bacon
1 tbsp. green onion
½ tsp. dill
1/8 tsp. pepper

Mix all but almonds. Chill overnight. Shape into a pinecone. Press almonds into cheese and refrigerate.

Ham Dip

2 pkg. cream cheese
3 tbsp. sour cream or mayonnaise
½ tbsp. mustard
1 tbsp. tabasco sauce
2 squirts lemon juice
1 can ham

Mix well and chill. Serve with bread or crackers.

Cheese Pumpkins

2 cups old cheese, grated
2 tbsp. minced onion flakes
2 tbsp. chili sauce
gherkins

Mix cheese, onion and chili by hand. Press firmly and roll into 1 inch balls. Refrigerate in flat container. Use ¼ piece of toothpick. Insert into sliced gherkin and insert into cheese ball.

Orange Cheese Spread

2 pkg. cream cheese
½ cup icing sugar
1 tbsp. grated orange peel
2 tbsp. Grand Marnier
2 tbsp. frozen orange juice concentrate

Mix until smooth and refrigerate. Can be used as a fruit dip or as a fancy sandwich filling.

Salads

Caesar Salad

½ tsp. crushed garlic
1 cup mayonnaise
1/3 cup olive oil
1/8 cup lemon juice
1/8 cup water
10 drops Worcestershire sauce

Mix all the ingredients together well. Refrigerate and add to salad before serving.

1 head Romaine lettuce
5 slices bacon crumbled
¼ cup red onion chopped
1/8 cup Parmesan cheese
1 cup croutons

Mix and top with dressing.

Taco Salad

1 lb. hamburger, browned, cooled and drained
1 head lettuce, shredded
2 cups cheddar cheese, shredded
2 tomatoes, chopped
1 bag Tacos crushed
1 small bottle catalina salad dressing

Mix everything together and serve.

Fluffy Salad

1 can fruit cocktail
1 can mandarin oranges
1 can pineapple tidbits
1 pkg. vanilla pudding powder
1 tub cool whip
1 small vanilla yogurt

Drain all the fruit well. Mix the pudding powder, cool whip and yogurt. Add the drained fruit and mix well. Refrigerate over night.

Broccoli Salad

4 cups broccoli, chopped
1 cup sunflower seeds
1 cup raisins
¾ cup miracle whip
¼ cup sugar
2 tbsp. vinegar
½ cup red onion
6 slices bacon, crumbled

Mix broccoli, sunflower seeds and raisins. In a separate bowl mix miracle whip, sugar and vinegar. Pour over broccoli. Top with red onions and bacon.

Sweet Strawberry Spinach Salad

10 cups torn spinach
2 cups sliced strawberries
½ cup red onion
½ cup cheddar cheese, shredded
¼ cup toasted almonds
¼ cup honey
1 cup mayonnaise
2 tsp. dill

Mix spinach, strawberries, onion, cheese and almonds. In a separate bowl mix honey, mayonnaise and dill. Pour over salad and serve immediately.

Mandarin Orange Salad

6 cups romaine lettuce
1 can mandarin oranges drained
¼ cup almond slices
3 tbsp. sugar
6 slices bacon, crumbled
3 tbsp. vinegar
¼ cup sugar
½ tsp. mustard
½ tsp. paprika
1 tbsp. oil

Mix vinegar, sugar, mustard and paprika and oil. In a pan heat the almonds and 3 tbsp. sugar until the sugar melts and coats the almonds. Mix lettuce, oranges, almonds and bacon. Mix in dressing and serve immediately.

Tomato Basil Dressing

2 tbsp. olive oil
2 tbsp. cider vinegar
1 tsp. onion salt
1 tsp. garlic salt
1 tbsp. basil
½ tbsp. sugar
¼ cup ketchup
¾ cup mayonnaise

Mix everything together and chill.

Caramel Apple Salad

6 Snickers bars, chopped
4 apples chopped
1 carton cool whip
1 package dry instant vanilla pudding

Mix everything together and refrigerate.

Cabbage Salad

1 head cabbage, shredded
5 green onions
2 pkg. instant noodles broken up
¾ cup slivered almonds
¼ cup butter
½ cup sunflower seeds

Dressing:
½ cup olive oil
tbsp. soy sauce
½ cup sugar
¼ cup vinegar

Mix dressing and set aside. Brown noodles, seeds and almonds in butter. Mix everything together and let stand 15 minutes before serving.

Mint Cucumber Salad

1 mint tea bag
½ cup vinegar
1 ½ tbsp. sugar
¼ cup sour cream
¼ cup plain yogurt
English cucumbers, peeled and sliced

Steep tea bag in vinegar for 15 minutes. Remove tea bag and add the rest of the ingredients. Chill at least 10 minutes before serving.

Potato Corn Salad

¼ cup Ranch dressing
¼ cup BBQ sauce
2 tbsp. Dijon mustard
3 pounds potatoes boiled and quartered
1 can corn
½ cup celery
1 red pepper
½ cup red onion
6 slices bacon crumbled
½ cup cheddar cheese

Mix dressing, BBQ sauce and mustard. Add all but bacon and cheese. Mix well. Sprinkle with cheese and bacon. Serve.

Mushroom Salad

1 head romaine lettuce
1 cup sliced mushrooms
1 yellow pepper
½ cup feta cheese
5 slices bacon
½ cup pine nuts
2 tbsp. honey
5 tbsp. cider vinegar
¼ cup oil
1 clove garlic
½ tsp. cayenne

In a large bowl mix the lettuce, mushrooms, pepper and feta. In another bowl mix honey, cider vinegar, oil, garlic and cayenne. Pour over salad and toss. Sprinkle with bacon and pine nuts.

Mango Salad

2 mangoes
1 head romaine lettuce
½ cup red onion
½ cup mozzarella cheese
¼ cup oil
¼ cup cider vinegar
1 tbsp. sugar
¼ tsp. dry mustard
½ tsp. poppy seeds
1/8 tsp. salt
1/8 tsp. pepper

Mix the lettuce, mangoes, onion, and cheese. In another bowl mix the oil, cider vinegar, sugar, dry mustard, poppy seeds, salt and pepper. Pour over lettuce, toss and serve.

BLT Salad

1 head lettuce
10 slices bacon
1 cup grape tomatoes
¼ cup cheddar cheese
¼ cup croutons
½ cup ranch salad dressing

Cook bacon until crisp and shred cheese. Mix all ingredients together and serve.

Cider Dressing

1 cup olive oil
¼ cup cider vinegar
¼ cup maple syrup
1 tsp. Dijon mustard
1 tsp. ketchup
2 cloves garlic
1 tsp. salt

Put all in a blender and mix well.

Soups

Broccoli Soup

1 minced onion
3 chopped carrots
2 cut up and peeled potatoes
2 small bay leaves
1 head broccoli, cut up
¼ tsp. celery powder
2 tsp. chicken soup base
¼ cup cheese whiz
1 cup milk
3 tbsp. flour
pepper to taste

Cover onions, potatoes and carrots with 4 quarts of water. Cook until tender. Add bay leaves, broccoli, celery powder, soup base and cheese whiz. Mix well. Mix milk and flour. Add to soup. Add pepper to taste.

Cold Cucumber Soup

1 large cucumber, peeled and chopped
1 tbsp. lemon juice
1 clove garlic, skinned and crushed
2 cups plain yogurt
2 tbsp. fresh chives
1 tbsp. fresh parsley
salt
pepper
paprika

Put all in blender. Blend until very smooth. Chill well.

Cinnamon Peach Soup

2 pounds ripe peaches
3 whole cloves
3 allspice berries
3 cardamon pods
2 cups orange juice
3 tbsp. lime juice
4 tbsp. honey
1 tsp. ground cinnamon
1 tsp. ground ginger
1 cup yogurt

Drop peaches in boiling water for 30 seconds. Rinse under cold water. Remove skin. Pit. Chop coarsely. Wrap cloves, allspice and cardamon in foil. Pierce with a fork. Combine peaches spice bundle, orange juice, lime juice, honey cinnamon and ginger in pot. Simmer 5-10 minutes. Remove spice bundle. Cool. Puree in blender. Just before serving, whisk in yogurt.

Ham Chowder

3 cups diced potatoes
½ cup diced onion
1 cup sliced carrots
1 ½ cups water
1 tsp. parsley flakes
1 ½ tsp. chicken bouillon
1 can creamed corn
1 can flaked ham, mashed
1 ½ cups milk
¼ cup cheese whiz

Cook the first 6 ingredients until vegetables are tender. Add corn, ham, milk and cheese. Heat stirring often.

Sweet Potato Soup

4 pounds sweet potatoes cooked and slightly mashed
8 cups water
1/3 cup butter
½ cup tomato sauce
2 tbsp. cream
2 tsp. salt
1/8 tsp. pepper
1 sprinkle thyme
1 cup cashew pieces

Put the mashed sweet potatoes into a large saucepan over medium heat. Add the remaining ingredients and stir to combine. When the soup begins to boil, reduce heat and simmer for 50-60 minutes.

Chicken Noodle Soup

12 cups water
1 chicken carcass
3 heaping tbsp. chicken soup base
2 cups uncooked egg noodles
2 cups carrots
2 cups celery
2 cups chicken

Boil chicken carcass in water for a minimum of 2 hours. Remove carcass. Add the rest of the ingredients. Simmer until noodles are cooked and carrots are tender.

Mushroom Soup

3 tbsp. butter
4 cups sliced fresh mushrooms
1/3 cup finely chopped green onion
3 tbsp. flour
3 cups milk
salt
pepper
nutmeg

Melt the butter in a saucepan. Add the mushrooms and green onions. Sauté until tender. Sprinkle flour over the mixture. Cook 1 minute stirring constantly. Gradually add milk. Cook until it thickens and comes to a boil. Add salt, pepper and nutmeg to taste.

Sauerkraut Soup

1 jar sauerkraut
1 – 1 ½ cups split peas
1-2 onions
butter
salt and pepper

Rinse sauerkraut with cold water. Put in a pot and cover with one inch water over top. Chop onion and put in. Add salt. Boil and turn down. Simmer 30 minutes. In a separate pot wash peas. Cover with water and cook on low heat until you can mash them. Add mashed peas to sauerkraut. Stir. Fry butter and onions in a separate pot. Top each bowl of soup with the fried butter and onions.

Hamburger Soup

1 lb. hamburger
1 onion, chopped
½ cup diced celery
1 red pepper
2 tsp. sugar
½ tsp. pepper
2 tsp. salt
dill to taste
2 cups raw potato
4 cups cabbage
4 carrots
1 cup green beans
1 cup corn
1 jar hot and spicy spaghetti sauce
1 bay leaf
½ tsp. thyme

28 oz tin tomatoes
1 tin tomato soup
6 cups hot water
2 tsp. beef bouillon

Brown beef and take off grease. Add all veggies and simmer until tender. Add rest. Dilute by adding more bouillon and water if needed.

Chicken Vegetable Chowder

1 tbsp. butter
1 onion finely chopped
1 clove garlic finely chopped
1 tsp. curry powder
2 large potatoes peeled and cubed
2 cups chicken stock
1 bag frozen california style vegetables
1 cup milk
2 cups chicken cooked and chopped
1 tsp. oregano
salt
pepper

Heat the butter in a large sauce pan. Sauté the onion, garlic and curry powder for 2 minutes. Add the chicken stock, potatoes and oregano. Bring to a boil. Reduce the heat to low and cover. Cook for 15 minutes. Add the frozen vegetables. Bring to a boil and cook for another 5 minutes. Add the milk and the chicken. Season with salt and pepper. Heat but do not bring to a boil.

Garlic Soup

¼ cup butter
2 tbsp. olive oil
3 large onions sliced
2 heads of garlic, separated and peeled
½ tsp. cumin
½ tsp. dry mustard
4-5 cups chicken stock
1 cup cream

Melt butter, add oil and sauté onions and garlic. Cover and cook gently on low heat for 1 hour. Add cumin and mustard with 2 cups of stock. Simmer for 10 minutes. Put in blender and puree. Put back in pot and add the rest of the ingredients. Heat to desired temperature and serve.

Borscht

3 or 4 pork chops (any cut)
Just a bit less than ½ a dutch oven of water
1 heaping tablespoon of chicken base
1 onion diced
1 cup shredded potatoes
1 cup shredded carrots
1 cup shredded beets and beet tops
1 can pork and beans
1 can peas and carrots and the liquid
2 tbsp. dill
1 cup whipping cream
½ cup sugar
1 can tomato soup
½ cup vinegar

Simmer the pork chops in just less than ½ a dutch oven of water and the soup base for 10 minutes. Add the onion, potato, carrots and beets. Simmer for 15 minutes. Add pork and beans, peas, carrots, dill, sugar and vinegar. Mix tomato soup and whipping cream until smooth. Add to soup. Add salt and pepper to taste.

CLOCKWISE FROM TOP LEFT: VEGETABLE PIZZA, BAKED BRUSCHETTA, HAM DIP, PARMESAN HAM SWIRLS, CHEESE PUMPKINS, TACO DIP

LEFT TO RIGHT BAVARIAN SCHNITZEL, SPAGHETTI PIE

Vegetables

Broth Vegetables

1/3 cup chicken broth
½ cup water
1 cup chopped carrots
1 cup cauliflower
1 cup broccoli

Boil vegetables in broth and water until they are tender.

Grilled Vegetables

3 zucchini
2 red peppers
2 yellow peppers
1 orange pepper
¼ cup parmesan cheese
¼ cup Italian salad dressing

Slice vegetables and barbeque. Toss with salad dressing and parmesan cheese.

New Potatoes

2 lbs. boiled new potatoes
¾ cup green onions chopped
½ cup butter
½ cup heavy cream
¼ cup fresh dill

Sauté onions and dill in butter. Add cream to sauce pan. Cook until thick. Pour over boiled potatoes.

Cheddar Mushrooms

30 mushroom caps
1 cup cheddar cheese
¼ cup bacon
2 tsp. parsley

Put mushrooms stem side up in a greased pan. Top with cheese and bacon. Sprinkle with parsley. Bake at 375F for 20 minutes.

Vegetable Casserole

broccoli
carrots
cauliflower
peas
2 tbsp. butter
2 tbsp. flour
½ tsp. salt
pepper
1 cup milk
½ pkg. cream cheese
1 cup shredded cheddar cheese
1 cup bread crumbs
2 tbsp. melted butter

Boil broccoli, cauliflower, carrots and peas. Drain and put in a greased 9x13 pan. Melt 2 Tbsp. butter in a pot. Add the next 4 ingredients. Stir until bubbly. Reduce heat and stir in cream cheese until blended. Pour over vegetables. Mix. Sprinkle cheddar cheese over the vegetables. Mix the bread crumbs and margarine. Top with this mixture. Bake at 350 F for 40 minutes.

Sweet and Sour Red Cabbage

1 red cabbage shredded
2 tbsp. vinegar
4 slices bacon crumbled
¼ cup brown sugar
1 minced onion
2 tbsp. flour
½ cup water
¼ cup vinegar
1 tsp. salt
1/8 tsp. pepper

In saucepan heat ½ inch salted water. Add 2 tbsp. vinegar when boiling. Add cabbage. Cover. Heat to boiling. Cool 5 minutes. Drain. Fry bacon in a pan. Pour off half the drippings. Add brown sugar and flour. Add ¼ cup vinegar, salt, pepper and onions. Cook until thick. Add bacon mixture to cabbage. Heat through.

Baked Sweet Potatoes

2 lbs. sweet potatoes, cooked and mashed
½ cup mayonnaise
¼ cup packed brown sugar
1 tbsp. orange juice
½ cup ginger snap crumbs
¼ cup sugar
¼ cup butter
¼ cup chopped pecans

Combine potatoes, mayonnaise, brown sugar and orange juice. Spoon into a casserole dish. Stir together the crumbs, sugar, butter and pecans. Sprinkle on top of potato mixture. Bake at 350 F for 30 minutes.

Cheesy Vegetable Casserole

½ lb. American cheese
½ cup butter
1 bag California vegetables, thawed and drained
1 cup crushed crackers

Cut cheese into cubes. Place in saucepan with ¼ cup butter. Heat, stirring until smooth. Place veggies in a casserole dish. Pour cheese sauce on and mix well. Melt butter and stir in cracker crumbs. Sprinkle over top. Bake 350 F for 20-25 minutes.

Bacon Garlic Potatoes

- 3 lbs. potatoes
- 8 slices bacon
- 2 cloves garlic
- 1 cup sour cream
- ¼ cup butter
- 1 tsp. salt
- ½ tsp. pepper
- ¼ cup chives
- 1 cup mozzarella cheese

Boil potatoes and fry bacon and garlic. Mix all ingredients together and mash. Put all in a casserole dish and bake at 350F for 20 minutes.

Fried Corn

2 – 16 ounce packages of whole kernel corn, frozen
1 stick butter (not margarine)
1 cup whipping cream
1 tbsp. sugar
1 tsp. salt

Put all in a skillet over medium heat. Stir constantly until most of the butter and whipping cream is absorbed into the corn.

Creamed Spinach

- 2 pkg. frozen spinach, cooked
- 2 pkg. cream cheese
- 3 tbsp. margarine
- 1 cup seasoned bread crumbs

Mix first 3 ingredients over heat until melted and mixed well. Put into a greased casserole dish. Top with bread crumbs. Bake at 350F for 15-20 minutes.

Zucchini Patties

1 ½ cups grated zucchini
1 egg beaten
2 tbsp. flour
1/3 cup onion
½ tsp. season salt

Mix all and fry on both sides. Serve with marinara sauce to dip.

Vegetable Stirfry

1 onion
1 red pepper
1 bag California vegetables
1 clove garlic
½ tsp. seasoned salt
1 tsp. tomato basil seasoning

In pan sauté onion, pepper and garlic until tender. Add rest and cook until hot.

Dilled Potatoes

4 baking potatoes
2 tsp. olive oil
½ tsp. seasoned salt
1 tsp. dill

Make slices part way through each potato to make a fan. Drizzle potatoes with oil. Sprinkle with seasoned salt and dill. Wrap in tin foil and bake at 350F until potatoes are tender.

Baked Beans

½ lb. bacon
½ lb. hamburger
½ cup onion
1 can kidney beans
1 can baked beans
1 tsp. salt
½ cup ketchup
¾ cup brown sugar
1 tsp. dry mustard

Brown bacon, hamburger and onions. Drain. Place in a casserole dish. Add the kidney and baked beans. In a bowl stir together salt, ketchup, brown sugar and dry mustard. Stir into beans. Bake at 350F for 2-3 hours.

Pasta

Fettuccine Alfredo

8 ounces Fettuccine noodles
½ cup Parmesan cheese
1/3 cup whipping cream
3 tbsp. butter
1 dash nutmeg
pepper

Cook pasta according to the package. Drain and return to the pot. Add cream, cheese butter. Mix well. Transfer to a serving dish. Sprinkle with nutmeg and pepper.

Manicotti

1 medium onion chopped
2 cups cooked ham, chopped
1 head broccoli chopped
salt
pepper
2 cups mozzarella cheese, grated
8 tubes manicotti
¼ cup butter   2 cups milk
¼ cup flour   1 jar pasta sauce

Sauté onions until tender. Add ham, broccoli and half the cheese. Season to taste with salt and pepper. Cook manicotti, rinse with cold water and stuff with ham mixture. Melt butter in a saucepan. Add flour. Cook stirring constantly until thick. Add remaining cheese. Stir until smooth. Season to taste. Spread pasta sauce in the bottom of a casserole dish. Arrange manicotti in sauce. Pour cheese sauce over manicotti. Sprinkle with Parmesan cheese. Bake at 375 F for 30 minutes.

Spaghetti Carbonara

¼ cup flour
¼ cup butter
2 cups milk
1/8 tsp. pepper
½ tsp. salt
24 slices bacon
¼ cup olive oil
2 cups mushrooms
4 tbsp. green onions
1 pound spaghetti, cooked
½ cup Parmesan cheese

Melt butter. Stir in flour. Add milk, salt and pepper. Heat, stirring until thick. Fry bacon, add to sauce. Heat oil. Add mushrooms and onions. Cook until golden. Add to sauce. Add spaghetti to sauce. Transfer to serving dish. Top with Parmesan cheese.

Fettuccine Primavera

cooked Fettuccine
1 cup broccoli
1 cup milk
1 pkg. cream cheese
4 green onions
½ tsp. Italian seasoning
¼ tsp. garlic powder
1 cup cubed chicken
½ cup Parmesan cheese

Cook pasta adding broccoli during last 5 minutes. Drain. Stir milk, cream cheese, seasonings and onions in saucepan on low heat until smooth. Stir in chicken and half of the Parmesan cheese. Toss pasta with vegetables and sauce. Top with the rest of the Parmesan cheese.

Spaghetti Sauce

1 large can tomato sauce
2 lbs. hamburger
1 onion, chopped
1 cup sliced mushrooms
1 tbsp. olive oil
2 tbsp. brown sugar
1 tbsp. soy sauce
2 red peppers, chopped
2 cups zucchini, chopped
1 tsp. basil
1 tsp. oregano
1 tsp. Italian seasoning

Fry hamburger and drain. Add oil, mushrooms, onion, peppers and zucchini. Sauté 5 minutes. Add soy sauce, brown sugar, tomato sauce, basil, oregano and Italian seasoning. Heat to serve.

No Boil Lasagna

1 tbsp. oil	mozzarella cheese
2 -14oz cans Tomato sauce	2 tsp. oil
1- 10 oz can sliced Mushrooms	1 egg
1 tsp. oregano	1 clove garlic
½ cup Water	½ pkg. lasagna noodles
1 cup Cottage cheese	1 lb. hamburger
1/3 cup Parmesan cheese	1 onion

Sauté onion and garlic in oil. Add ground beef and brown. Remove excess fat. Stir in tomato sauce, mushrooms with their liquid, water and oregano. Bring to a boil. Remove from heat and set aside. Combine cottage cheese, Parmesan cheese, egg, oil and salt. Set aside. Spoon 1/3 meat sauce in 9x13 pan. Cover with 1/3 of the lasagna noodles. Spread another 1/3 of meat sauce. Cover with noodles. Spread cottage cheese mixture over noodles and cover with remaining noodles and sauce. Top with mozzarella cheese. Cover with foil and bake at 375 F for 45 minutes. Uncover and bake until cheese starts to brown, 15 minutes.

Spinach Fettuccine

1 package chopped spinach
¾ lb. fettuccine
2 tbsp. margarine
1 chopped onion
2 cloves minced garlic
1 ½ tsp. dried basil
3 tbsp. flour
2 ¼ cups milk
1 cup Parmesan cheese
3 tbsp. tomato paste
¼ tsp. ground nutmeg
pinch cayenne pepper
¾ tsp. salt

Cook pasta. Melt margarine in a saucepan. Add onion, garlic and basil. Cook 3-5 minutes. Stir in flour. Gradually whisk in milk making sure that there is no lumps. Bring to a boil. Reduce heat. Simmer 1 minute. Stir in spinach, ½ cup Parmesan cheese, tomato paste, salt nutmeg and cayenne pepper. Toss with fettuccine. Serve with the remaining Parmesan cheese sprinkled on top.

Chicken Caesar Pasta

1 tbsp. oil
1 lb. cubed chicken
1 can cream of celery soup
½ cup water
1/3 cup Caesar salad dressing
4 cups cooked linguine
1 diced tomato
1/8 tsp. pepper
Parmesan cheese

Heat oil and brown chicken. Stir in soup, water and salad dressing. Heat to boil, stirring occasionally. Cover and cook over low heat until chicken is cooked through. Toss with linguine and tomato. Sprinkle with pepper and Parmesan cheese.

Meats

Tahitian Chicken

¼ cup margarine
½ cup brown sugar
1 package onion soup mix
2 tbsp. cornstarch
1 tin pineapple chunks
2 tbsp. lemon juice
½ cup water
chicken pieces

Mix first 4 ingredients in a saucepan. Heat until margarine melts. Add pineapple, lemon and water. Pour over chicken. Bake at 350 F until done.

Chicken with Ham and Cheese

6 boneless skinless chicken breasts
¼ cup flour
seasoning salt
butter for frying
6 slices ham
6 slices mozzarella cheese

Mix flour and seasoning salt. Dip chicken in flour. Brown both sides. Bake at 350 F for 7 minutes. Place ham then cheese on each chicken breast. Return to oven until cheese melts to golden.

Oven Ribs

2 tbsp. vegetable oil
1 large minced onion
¼ cup brown sugar
¾ cup ketchup
¼ cup lemon juice
1 tbsp. Dijon mustard
1 tbsp. Worcestershire sauce
1 tsp. chili powder
4 pounds spare ribs

Pre cook ribs in shallow roasting pan for 30 minutes at 450 F. Heat oil in small saucepan. Cook onion until soft. Stir in brown sugar until dissolved. Remove form heat. Stir in rest of ingredients. Pour sauce over ribs. Continue roasting for 1 hour at 350 F.

CLOCKWISE FROM TOP LEFT: NEW POTATOES, CHICKEN MARSEILLES, VEGETABLE BEEF STIRFRY, BACON GARLIC POTATOES, FRIED CORN, BROCCOLI SALAD, CHICKEN BACON STEW

LEFT TO RIGHT: ROASTED PEPPER AND ONION DIP, GUACAMOLE, CHICKEN ENCHILADAS

Sloppy Joes

1 lb. ground beef
1 small onion minced
1 tsp. salt
1/8 tsp. pepper
¼ tsp. chili powder
2 tbsp. flour
½ tsp. Worcestershire sauce
¾ cup ketchup

Cook beef, spices and onions until meat loses its red colour. Blend in flour. Add 1 ¼ cups water, ketchup, and Worcestershire sauce. Simmer 15-20 minutes.

Chicken Rolls

1 cup sharp cheddar cheese grated
1 tbsp. water
1 tsp. dried onion
1/8 tsp. crushed tarragon
4 boneless skinless chicken breasts halved lengthwise
3 tbsp. butter melted

Combine first 4 ingredients. Set aside. Pound chicken to 1/8 of an inch thickness. Salt and pepper both sides. Divide cheddar mixture among chicken. Fold in sides. Roll up like a jellyroll. Close with toothpicks. Place on baking sheet. Brush with butter. Broil 15 minutes. Turn. Broil 15 more minutes.

Stuffed Chicken Rolls

1 chicken bouillon cube
2/3 cup boiling water
2 cups packaged bread stuffing
½ cup cooked chopped broccoli
4 chicken breasts boned flattened and split
½ cup flour   ½ tsp. paprika
¼ tsp. celery salt   dash of pepper
3 tbsp. butter   1 tsp. parsley
1 ½ tsp. toasted sesame seeds
2 tbsp. soy sauce
2 tbsp brown sugar
2/3 cup pineapple juice

Dissolve bouillon in boiling water. Add to stuffing with broccoli and parsley. Place stuffing on each chicken half. Roll up and fasten with toothpicks. Dredge in flour mixed with seasonings. Brown in butter. Arrange chicken in a baking dish. Add rest of ingredients to drippings in skillet. Bring to boiling point. Pour over chicken. Bake at 375 F for 45 minutes.

Barbeque Rib Sauce

1 cup ketchup
1 cup red wine vinegar
½ cup brown sugar
¼ cup molasses
1 ½ tsp. liquid smoke
½ tsp. salt
rounded ¼ tsp. pepper
¼ tsp. garlic powder
¼ tsp. onion powder

Combine and heat over high heat and whisk until smooth. Bring to a boil. Simmer uncovered 30-40 minutes until thickened.

Hawaiian Pork

1 pound pork
2 eggs
1 green pepper
¼ tsp. pepper
1 can chicken broth
½ cup pineapple chunks drained
½ cup pineapple juice
2 ½ tbsp. cornstarch
½ cup sugar
3 tbsp. soy sauce
1/3 cup vinegar

¼ cup flour
1 tsp. salt
½ cup oil
4 celery stalks

Cube pork. Beat egg with flour, salt and pepper. Heat oil in a heavy pan. Dip pork in batter and drop into oil and brown. Cube celery and green pepper. Add vegetables, ¼ cup broth, Pineapple and juice. Cover and simmer 15 minutes. Combine cornstarch and sugar. Blend in soy sauce, vinegar, and rest of broth. Cook until clear over medium heat. Pour over meat and simmer 5 minutes.

Bavarian Schnitzel

1 pound pork tenderloin
¼ cup flour
1 egg
1 tbsp. water
2 cups bread crumbs
1 tsp. thyme
½ tsp. salt
¼ tsp. pepper
2 tbsp. butter
2 tbsp. oil

Pound pork tenderloin thin. Gently beat egg with water. Combine breadcrumbs with thyme, salt and pepper. One by one dip pork in flour, then egg, then breadcrumbs. Place on a wire rack and refrigerate for 30-60 minutes. Heat oil in a large frying pan over medium heat. When hot add butter. Sauté pork until golden brown and cooked through.

Rootbeer Chicken

1 ½ cups rootbeer
1 ½ cups ketchup
2 tbsp. Worcestershire sauce
2 tbsp. onion
1 clove garlic
¼ tsp. hot sauce
1 roasting chicken or chicken pieces

Mix rootbeer, ketchup, worcestershire sauce, onion, garlic and hot sauce. Simmer for 30 minutes until thick. Brush over a roasting chicken every 20 minutes until chicken is cooked through.

Pineapple Ribs

3 lbs ribs
¾ cup plum sauce
1/3 cup frozen pineapple concentrate
1 tsp. ginger
2 tbsp. cider vinegar
½ tsp. salt
¼ cup lemon lime soda

Boil ribs. Mix plum sauce, pineapple concentrate, ginger, cider vinegar, salt and soda. Add boiled ribs and marinate for at least 1 hour. Grill or broil ribs brushing with marinade.

Coffee Spiced Steak

4 steaks
3 tsp. instant coffee
2 tsp. sugar
1 tsp. pepper
1 tsp. salt
1 ½ tsp. cinnamon
¼ tsp. allspice
4 tsp. olive oil

Mix the coffee, sugar, pepper, salt, cinnamon and allspice. Brush steaks with oil and rub on spice mix. Barbeque or broil steak.

Honey Garlic Tenderloin

2 tenderloins
½ cup soy sauce
2 cloves garlic
1 tsp. ginger
¼ cup honey
2 tbsp. brown sugar

Mix soy sauce, garlic, ginger, honey and brown sugar. Marinate tenderloins in sauce for at least 2 hours. Place tenderloin on a roasting pan and pour marinade over top. Bake at 350F for 40 minutes or until tenderloin is cooked through.

Chicken in Garlic Bread

16 boneless skinless chicken thighs
¾ cup butter
2 cloves garlic
½ cup flour   1 tbsp. dill
2 tsp. salt   ½ cup green onions
½ tsp. pepper
1 ½ tsp. paprika
1 loaf unsliced bread
½ cup butter
2 tbsp. sun dried tomatoes in oil

Mix flour, salt, pepper and paprika. Coat chicken in flour mixture. Melt ¾ cup butter in a baking dish. Add chicken and bake at 450F for 30 minutes. In a pan melt ½ cup butter. Add tomatoes, dill, onion and garlic. Saute 5 minutes. Cut top off bread and remove filling. Brush inside of bread with garlic mixture. Pack chicken inside and wrap in foil. Bake at 400F for 1 hour.

Beef and Garlic Stir Fry

2 tbsp. oil
1 lb. steak cut in strips
1 onion sliced thinly
2 cloves garlic, minced
1 can condensed beef broth
1-2 tbsp. soy sauce
2 tbsp. cornstarch
3 cups frozen vegetables
4 cups cooked rice

Heat oil and brown beef. Add onion and garlic, stir-fry 3 minutes. Drain fat. Stir in consommé, Soya sauce, and cornstarch. Heat to a boil. Reduce heat. Add vegetables and simmer until cooked through. Serve over rice.

Coke BBQ Sauce

2 medium onions
¾ cup coke
¾ cup ketchup
2 tbsp. vinegar
2 tbsp. Worcestershire sauce
½ tsp. chili powder
½ tsp. salt

Mince onions. Combine all ingredients and bring to a boil. Reduce heat and simmer 45 minutes.

Quick Pork Chops

4 pork chops
¼ cup ketchup
¼ cup water
¼ cup brown sugar
½ cup chopped onion
4 lemon slices
½ tsp. garlic
seasoned salt

Place chops in sprayed pan. Sprinkle with seasoned salt. Mix ketchup, water, brown sugar and garlic together. Pour over chops. Sprinkle with chopped onion. Place a slice of lemon on each pork chop. Cover and bake at 350 F for 1 ½ hours.

Dancing Chicken

1 whole chicken
1 can beer
Chicken seasoning

Put your favorite spices on the chicken and rub it into the skin. Open the beer can and put it upright in the chickens' cavity. It is best to do this over a foil-covered pan. Put the chicken standing up in the BBQ for 1 ¼-1 ½ hours.

Dancing Chicken Seasoning

Mix seasoned salt, pepper, oregano, basil, parsley, thyme, celery salt, onion salt, paprika and garlic powder. Rub on outside of chicken and BBQ.

Chicken Linguine

- 1 tbsp. olive oil
- 1 onion
- 1 red pepper
- 1 can mushrooms
- 1/3 cup chicken broth
- 2 tbsp. red wine vinegar
- 1 can tomato sauce
- 2 cloves garlic
- ¼ tsp. salt
- ¼ tsp. pepper
- 1 lb. chicken cut into cubes
- 2 tsp. basil
- Linguine
- parsley
- Parmesan cheese

Heat oil in skillet. Sauté onion, pepper and mushrooms until tender. Add broth and vinegar. Add tomato sauce, garlic, sugar, salt, pepper, chicken and basil. Add Parmesan cheese and parsley. Serve over linguine.

Chicken Marseilles

3 tbsp. margarine
5-6 chicken breasts
1 pkg. vegetable soup dip and mix
½ tsp. dill
½ cup sour cream

Melt margarine in skillet and brown chicken. Stir in 2 cups water, soup mix and dill. Bring to a boil. Reduce heat and simmer. Stir occasionally for 25-30 minutes or until chicken is tender. Remove chicken and stir in sour cream until creamy. Pour sauce over chicken and serve with rice.

Ham Sauce

1 cup brown sugar
2 tsp. dry mustard
3 tbsp. corn starch
4 tbsp. vinegar
1-2 cups pineapple juice

Thicken. Pour over ham and cook.

BBQ Pork and Apples

2 tbsp. olive oil
2 tbsp. cider vinegar
2 tbsp. vinegar
½ tsp. thyme
¼ tsp. salt
¼ tsp. pepper
1 lb. pork
4 apples
¼ cup water
2 tsp. lemon juice

Mix oil, vinegar, mustard and spices. In another bowl mix water and lemon juice. Cut apples in four pieces. Dip in lemon water. Cut pork in cubes. Thread alternating on skewers. Brush oil mixture over skewers and grill until meat is cooked through and apples are soft.

Chicken Enchiladas

½ cup mayonnaise
½ cup flour
3 cups milk
1 pkg. tex mex cheese
5 cups shredded chicken
¾ cups salsa
16 flour tortillas

Heat oven to 375 F. Mix mayonnaise and flour in a pan. Add milk and cook until thick. Stir in half the cheese. Reserve 1 cup of the cheese sauce. Add the chicken and salsa. Place sauce down middle of each tortilla and roll up. Put in a 9x13 pan seam side down. Top with the rest of the cheese sauce and shredded cheese. Bake for 25 minutes uncovered.

Spaghetti Pie

1 cup chopped cooked chicken
1 jar alfredo sauce
5 cups cooked spaghetti
1 jar spaghetti sauce
2 cups shredded cheese

Heat oven to 350F. In a 9x13 pan spread the jar of alfredo sauce in the bottom. Place spaghetti on top. Mix chicken and spaghetti sauce. Place over spaghetti. Top with cheese. Bake covered for 30 minutes.

Index

A
Amaretto spread 33

B
Bacon cheeseball 35
Bacon dip 29
Bacon garlic potatoes 74
Bacon log 27
Baked beans 79
Baked bruschetta 15
Baked cream cheese 25
Baked sweet potatoes 72
Barbeque rib sauce 98
Bavarian schnitzel 100
BBQ pork and apples 113
BBQ water chestnuts 9
Beef garlic stir fry 106
BLT salad 51
Borscht 64
Brie en croute 26
Broccoli salad 42
Broccoli soup 53
Broth vegetables 68

C
Cabbage salad 46
Caesar salad 39
Caramel apple brie 33
Caramel apple salad 45
Cashew wafers 34
Cheddar beer spread 23
Cheddar dill loaf 17

Cheddar mushrooms 69
Cheese pumpkins 36
Cheese sticks 32
Cheeseball 11
Cheesy vegetable casserole 73
Cherry puffs 19
Chestnut surprises 28
Chicken Caesar pasta 88
Chicken enchiladas 114
Chicken in garlic bread 105
Chicken linguine 110
Chicken Marseilles 111
Chicken noodle soup 58
Chicken rolls 96
Chicken vegetable chowder 62
Chicken with ham and cheese 91
Cider dressing 51
Cinnamon peach soup 55
Coconut dip 24
Coffee spiced steak 103
Coke BBQ sauce 107
Cold cucumber soup 54
Creamed spinach 76

D

Dancing chicken 109
Dancing chicken seasoning 109
Dilled potatoes 78

F

Fettuccine alfredo 81
Fettuccine prima vera 84
Fluffy salad 41
Fried corn 75

G

Garlic soup 63
Grilled vegetables 68
Guacamole 14

H

Ham chowder. 56
Ham dip 35
Ham sauce 112
Hamburger soup 61
Hawaiian pork 99
Honey garlic tenderloin 104
Hot artichoke dip 22
Hot broccoli dip 17
Hot pumpernickel dip 10
Hot spinach loaf 30

K

Kahlua dip 16

M

Mandarin orange salad 44
Mango salad 50
Manicotti 82
Mint cucumber salad 47
Mozzarella dip 31
Mushroom salad 49
Mushroom soup 59

N

New potatoes 69
No boil lasagna 86

O

Orange cheese spread 37
Oven ribs 92

P

Parmesan ham swirls 18
Peanut butter dip 26
Pineapple ribs 102
Potato corn salad 48

Q

Quick pork chops 108

R

Roasted pepper and onion dip 16
Rootbeer chicken 101

S

Sauerkraut soup 60
Sloppy Joes 95
Spaghetti carbonara 83
Spaghetti pie 115
Spaghetti sauce 85
Spinach and artichoke dip 13
Spinach dip 24
Spinach fettuccine 87
Stuffed chicken rolls 97
Sweet and sour red cabbage 71
Sweet potato soup 57
Sweet strawberry spinach salad 43

T

Taco dip 8
Taco salad 40

Tahitian chicken 90
Tomato basil dressing 45

V

Vegetable casserole 66
Vegetable pizza 12
Vegetable stirfry 77

Z

Zucchini patties 77